PEARLS OF POETRY

VIBHU

To Ajja, my Guru

Contents

Foreword

When I was asked to write a foreword for this wonderful book of poems by Vibhu, I was wondering what to write that doesn't eclipse the beauty and splendor in the poems that grace these pages that follow. It is a tough ask.

I have known Vibhu since her childhood and she is blessed to have a free spirit that is soaked in imagination and devotion. This short book contains poems of rare depth and sublime beauty. The theme is clearly philosophical, but expressed in simple language with a lovely rhythm to it. It is the cry of a pure innocent heart to the One Divinity - the Infinity and Beyond.

Bharath, or India, is known to be the land where more than 33 crore Gods and Goddesses are worshipped by its people. However, it is only a pure innocent child like Vibhu that can see the one single unity amidst all this diversity. The first poem "HariHara" brilliantly captures the 'non-difference' of Hari and Hara. The concluding poem in this anthology beautifully describes the birth of Krishna. In between these two, you have splendid poems on Kali, Andal, Shiva and Shakti.

Each poem is a treat to the soul - as you read them you are taken on a pilgrimage with beautiful vistas of melodious forms and eddies of supernal bliss in an ocean of devotion.

-Nithin Nagaraj

(Professor at National Institute of Advanced Studies (NIAS), Indian Institute of Science (IISc.))

Preface

When I was younger, my paternal grandfather, whom I affectionately called "Ajja," would share spiritual and religious teachings with my sister and me. He often listened to Carnatic bhajans and even tried to teach us a few. I didn't realize it back then but these moments not only fostered a deep bond but also nurtured my love for Carnatic music and kindled a spiritual inclination from an early age.

In 2024, I encountered Bharatanatyam exponent Harinie Jeevitha and her book, *Perspectives*. Her graceful performances and the captivating beauty of her words left a profound impact on me. Inspired by her artistry and insights, I decided to try my hand at poetry.

Drawing from the teachings imparted by my Ajja, I began weaving religious and philosophical themes into poems. To my surprise, the results were beyond what I had imagined. Initially, I doubted whether poetry was my forte, but as inspiration struck and ideas flowed, I started penning them down. I also began to find inspiration for my poems in Carnatic compositions. The depth, beauty, and spirituality of those pieces resonated with me and provided countless themes for my poems. Over the course of a year, I compiled a collection of fourteen poems. It felt as though Devi Saraswati herself had made her presence known, guiding me through this creative expedition.

Throughout this journey, Hillary Maliakal, my English teacher, has been a tremendous source of support. She read my poems carefully and always offered thoughtful, constructive feedback that helped me grow as a writer. I would like to thank her for her support and guidance.

Looking back, it feels surreal to have gone from doubting my abilities to publishing a collection of poetry. This endeavor would not have been possible without the unwavering support of my parents, teachers—both formal and informal—friends, and everyone who stood by me during the making of this book. I owe them my heartfelt gratitude.

-Vibhu

Acknowledgements

Dear reader,

Many people have consciously and unconsciously helped in bringing my gift of poetry out.

Firstly, I would like to thank Devi Saraswati for giving me the knowledge and gift of writing. I firmly believe she makes her presence known through my poetry. It is through her grace that I am able to pen down my thoughts in the form of poems.

Secondly, I would like to thank Ajja, my grandfather, who I consider my Guru since it is through him I was religiously inclined from a young age. Although he sadly passed away in May of 2023, his memories will forever stay with me and his values and stories have taken form of poetry through me.

Thirdly, I would like to thank my parents, who have been my primary supporters since the beginning. They recognized my interest in literature early on and have been encouraging my poetry in recent times.. They appreciate my work and give corrections when and where it is needed.

I would like to extend my heartfelt thanks to my uncle, Professor Nithin Nagaraj from NIAS, IIS Bangalore, and also to my grandmother. My uncle has generously shared his spiritual insights with me, which have proven immensely beneficial in various aspects of my life. Both he and my grandmother have consistently shown appreciation for my poetry, offering encouragement and occasionally expressing surprise at the depth of maturity they find in my work. Their unwavering support has been invaluable, bolstering my confidence and motivating me to continuously improving my skills.

Lastly, I extend my heartfelt thanks to Kumari Harinie Jeevitha, a renowned Bharatanatyam exponent from Chennai. Her book 'Perspectives,' illustrated by Kumari Meghna Unnikrishnan, inspired me to venture into poetry, transforming my belief that it wasn't for me. This book profoundly changed my perspective, making me a dedicated poet.

Image Credits and Disclaimer

All images in this book are sourced from public domains or online platforms where the original creators are not specified. We extend our gratitude to these unknown artists for their work. If you recognize any image and can provide information about its creator, please contact us so we can provide proper credit. No copyright infringement is intended. If you are the rightful owner of any image and do not wish for it to be used, please contact the publisher for acknowledgment or removal.

Publisher Acknowledgment

I extend my sincere appreciation to Notion Press for their exceptional support and guidance in bringing this collection to life.

Their comprehensive publishing services and dedication to authors have been instrumental in transforming my manuscript into a published work. Their commitment to empowering writers has made this journey both seamless and rewarding.

-Vibhu

Prologue

Dear reader,

What lies ahead is a collection of fourteen poems, each one written with a heart full of devotion to the Divine, and with the blessings of the Divine guiding my hand. These poems are a reflection of my own spiritual journey, a humble attempt to express the awe and wonder I feel in the presence of something greater than myself.

As you read, I hope you find something that resonates with your own experiences and thoughts. May these words offer you a moment of reflection and perhaps even a deeper connection to the Divine, however you understand it. This is my journey, shared with you, and I invite you to explore it with me.

1. HariHara

The dual representation of Lord Vishnu (Hari) and Lord Shiva (Hara)

Between the one,

Who wears a snake as an ornament

And the one,

Who sleeps upon a snake,

I see no difference

Between the one,

With long matted hair

And the one,

With dark curly hair,

I see no difference

Between the one, who dances to the beat of *damru*

And the one,

Who makes the *gopis* sway to his venu,

I see no difference

Between the one,

Who decorates his head with the moon

And the one,

Who adorns his crown with a peacock feather,

I see no difference

Between the one,

Who is formless

And the one,

With the most attractive form,

I see no difference

Between the one,

Whose power is *Shakti*

And the one,

Whose other half is *Radha*

I see no difference

Between the one

Who is the colour of camphor

And the one,

who is the colour of dark storm clouds,

I see no difference

Between the one,

Whose *Tandav* evokes destruction
And the one,
Whose *Raas Leela* evokes love
I see no difference
Between the one
Who resides on *Kailasha*
And the one,
Who is the Lord of *Seshachalam*
I see no difference
Between the one
Who wears the skin of tigers
And the one,
Who is adorned in *pitambari*
I see no difference
Finally between
Hari and *Hara*
I see no difference
For they are the Supreme power

- This poem has been written to express my thoughts on the one God we all worship. Although the forms are different, in the end it is the Cosmic power we all believe in. Gods and deities have been made to tone down the complexity of that Cosmic power and to make it understandable for humans. Some may agree and some may not but it is their point of view which I cannot change.

2. Kalliyankattu Neeli

In the dead of the moonlight,
The tall trees whisper her tales
She roams the forest
With her unkempt locks
Clad in a white saree
Her laugh haunting
As she serves justice
To those who are wronged
Her fury burning like ember
As she waits upon trees
Baring her fangs
Her eyes bloodshot
As she brutally avenges
Those who wronged her
In the guise of a petite woman
She appears to men
Who abuse and betray
She traps them with deceit
And lures them to their end
Her tale a remainder
To those who
Mock a woman's power
She doesn't succumb

To the patriarchal norms
For she is a rebel,
A free- spirit
Who cannot be tamed
She is NEELI

- The legend of *Kalliyankattu Neeli* is one of the most haunting and popular folktales in Kerala. The story revolves around Neeli, a woman who was wronged and became a vengeful spirit after her death.
- This poem is quite different to the other poems specifically because it doesn't focus on religion but rather a folktale. This poem did make me step out of my comfort zone, and I have tried my best to capture the folklore into a poem.

3. Swans of Saraswati

Painting of Devi Sarawati by Raja Ravi Verma

In the realm of Lord *Brahma*,
You reside, Oh! *Mahashveta*!
Pure and bright,
Clad in white,

Oh! *Sharade*, with a radiant light,
Stringing the veena
With your tender hands,
Emitting waves of cosmic tunes.
Oh! *Gyanapradayani*,
Bless me with the thirst for knowledge.
Oh! *Hamsavahini*,
Your swans, snowy white,
With grace, they glide
Through waters clear and still.
Oh! *Varapradayani*,
Bless me with your brilliance,
Remove the blanket of ignorance
That blinds me in worldly life.
Oh! *Vidyarupini*,
Help me fight
The demons of darkness
That plague my innocent mind.
Oh! *Gayatri*,
I surrender to Your lotus feet,
Guide me and grant me
Wisdom and knowledge
Of the arts and sciences,
Which shall guide me
Through times good and bad.

- My entry into the world of poetry has been made possible through the blessings of *Devi Saraswati*. As the goddess of knowledge and wisdom, she has guided me and will continue guiding me on this beautiful journey.

4. The Ever-Elusive Krishna

Painting of Maa Yashoda with Sri Krishna

Oh *Kannaiya*, where are you?

Don't you see all the garlands I offer?

Or the colourful fragrant flowers?

Why must you torment me like this?

It it the delicious curd you want?

Or milk of cows?

Kanna, show me your beautiful form

I've searched for you everywhere,

On the banks of *Yamuna,*

In the temples of *Vrindavan*

And the green *Govardhana*

But you don't show yourself

Where are you? Oh *Krishna*!

Your devotee calls you desperately

Shouldn't you come running?

Is it *Yashode* who keeps you from coming?

Or do the *gopikas* hold you back?

Suddenly I see you everywhere

But catching you isn't easy

Why do you vanish in the blink of an eye?

Naradar tells me stories of your greatness,

Garuda sings your praises,

Anantashesha serves you,

Reward my service and devotion

Kannaiya, show me your beautiful form

Sway me with melodies of your flute

For the birds, deers and cows admire it too

The peacocks dance in the rain

To the tunes of your flute

Kannaiya, I surrender myself at your Lotus feet,

For I cannot bear this separation from you

- This poem describes the agony of a devotee who cannot bear separation from *Sri Krishna*. The devotee calls out to him desperately, tries to find him in all possible places. The devotee questions him about what or who is stopping him and praises him. But *Sri Krishna* is ever elusive. Only after the devotee surrenders completely to him does he finally show himself.

5. The Union of Sri and Hari

Painting depicting Lakshmi (Sri) and Narayan (Hari) in His abode Vaikuntha

As the moon rises,
Higher in the night sky,
Krishna plays his flute
The tunes he weaves
Reach *Radha*'s ears
It's a sign to meet him,
Under the starry sky

By the serene *Yamuna*

Her anklets jingle merrily

As she runs past,

The glistening waters

To meet the one who charms Her

As He calls out to Her

The moonlight bathes them

When their longing eyes meet

He enchants His dear

With the melodies of his flute

He dances with her

In pure love and ecstasy

In the heavens above,

The Gods and Goddesses

Watch the play of the divine

Feeling blessed to witness

The union of *Sri* and *Hari*

In the divine forms

Of *Radha* and *Krishna*

- *Hari* is another name for *Vishnu/Krishna* meaning 'the one who takes away all sorrows, pains and sins' whereas, *Sri* is another name for *Lakshmi/Radha* meaning 'auspicious or wealth'.

- The poem is inspired by '*Radha Madhava Samvadam*' an excerpt from a Bharatanatyam recital '*Leela Taranga Margam*' by *Sridevi Nrithyalaya*. It describes the divine pastimes of *Sri Krishna* along with *Sri Radha.*

6. Call of Vitthala

**Sri Vitthal and Sri Rukmini in the Sri Vitthal Rukmini
Mandir in Pandharpur, Maharashtra**

When the Lord of *Pandharpur* calls,

Devotees fill the roads

Marching with devotion

Through sunshine and rain

Barefoot they march

With *Tulsi* plants

Carefully balanced on their heads
As they make their way along
With *Dnyaneshwar** from *Alandi*
And *Tukaram** from *Dehu*
In beautifully decorated palanquins
They carry the divine *padukas* (footprints)
Of the two eternal devotees
As they make their way through
The sea of devotees rejoicing
Dancing in delight
And singing *Abhangas*
The Lord waits patiently
Standing upon a brick
For the arrival of his devotees
As they reach the abode
Of *Vithoba*** and *Rakhumai***
Dnyaneshwar and *Tukaram****
Finally meet their Lord
Shedding tears of ecstasy
They pay their respects
And sing his praises
Thus, comes the pilgrimage to an end
The devotees reunited
With *Vitthala* and *Rukmini*

- *Sant Dnyaneshwar* (13th century) and *Sant Tukaram* (17th century) are two of the most popular devotees of *Lord*

Vitthala. They both are credited to writing numerous Abhangs or bhajans in praise of *Lord Vitthala*.

- **Vithoba is another name given to *Narayan avatar Vitthal*, who is the Lord of *Pandharpura, Maharashtra*. He resides in *Pandharpur* alongside his divine consort *Lakshmi avatar Rukmini* also known as *Rakhumai*.

- ***I imagine *Sant Dnyaneshwar* and *Sant Tukaram* finally meeting their Lord after a long journey from *Alandi* and *Dehu* respectively to see the Lord himself. They sing his praises through *Abhangs* as they are reunited with *Vithoba*.

- This poem is inspired by the *Palkhi* processions that took place on 2nd July 24 in Pune. I have tried my best to capture the culture and devotion into a poem but I firmly believe I can never do justice to the same. Any mistakes or inaccuracies are regretted.

7. The Beginning of the Universe

An artwork depicting Shiva and Parvati's divine dance 'Lasya Tandav'

Before the Universe,
There was eternal void
Unending and infinite

With the beat of *damru*,
Shiva starts His Cosmic dance
With His divine consort *Shakti*
The five elements are formed
Giving birth to the world
The rivers flow steadfast,
Fruit bearing trees sprout,
The birds chirp merrily in their nests,
The blue skies are created
Shakti, Who is Nature herself,
Nurtures the creatures
Shiva, Who is the Universe himself
Merges with Shakti,
To protect the beautiful world
To ponder deeply,
In this vast world,
Our physical forms are nothing,
But mere puppets
In the play of the Divine
In simpler words,
When the Divine says,
Let there be a void,
There is Nothing,
When the Divine says,
Let there be life,
The Universe is created
Just as the Divine embraces

The beginning of the Universe,
We, humans must embrace
New beginnings in our lives

- This poem was initially written for the school newsletter upon the request of my English teacher. But for me, my gift of poetry is a way of worship. Hence I have included this poem along with the others.

- This poem describes the beginning of the Universe as per the *Shaiva* sect (or the people who worship *Shiva* as their main deity) of *Hinduism* who believe *Shiva* created the Universe.

- This poem is my interpretation on the beginning of the world where *Lord Shiva* and *Goddess Parvati* perform the *Lasya Tandav*. *Lasya* is the style of dance representing the divine feminine and *Tandav* is the style of dance representing the divine masculine.

- As per my interpretation when *Lord Shiva* and *Goddess Parvati* perform the divine dance, the elements are created which give birth to our Universe.

- **Disclaimer**: This poem does not claim any Puranic backing and hence is a work of imagination.

8. Praise of Sri Vishnu

**A painting depicting the 'Chaturbhuj' (four armed) form
of Sri Vishnu**

I pray to Him,

Who is the Lord of the Universe,

The one who is dutiful,

In preserving the Universe (1)

I submit to Him,

Who lies upon **Anantashesha**,

Who dwells in **Vaikuntam**,

Who resides upon the **Kshira Sagara** (2)

I worship Him,

Who's divine consort is *Sri*,

The Goddess of wealth,

Who resides on the pink Lotus (3)

I praise Him,

Who is the enchanter of *Radha*,

Who plays his melodious flute,

By the steadfast holy **Yamuna** (4)

I admire Him,

Who is as **dark as the storm clouds**,

Who is adorned in **Pitambari**

Who wields the mighty **Sudarshana** (5)

I adore Him,

Who playfully steals butter,

Who is tied to the mortar,

By the oblivious **Mother Yashoda** (6)

1. The first stanza speaks about how *Sri Vishnu* is the Lord of the Universe (*Jaganatha*), how he dutifully preserves the Universe when it is wronged by *Adharma* or the unrighteous.

2. The second stanza speaks about *Sri Vishnu*'s abode (*Vaikumtam*), where he lies upon *AnantaSesha*, a snake with five heads which resides upon the *Kshira Sagara* or

Ocean of Milk which symbolises stability and continuity in the Universe.

3. The third stanza speaks about *Sri Vishnu's* divine consort *Sri*, Who is also known as *Devi Lakshmi*. She is the Goddess of wealth and prosperity. She resides upon the pink lotus which symbolises purity.

4. The fourth stanza speaks about *Sri Vishnu's Krishna avatar*. As *Krishna, Sri Vishnu* enchants His consort *Devi Lakshmi* who has taken the form of *Radha*. His divine pastimes include playing his melodious flute by the river *Yamuna*.

5. The fifth stanza speaks about *Sri Vishnu's* description. His skin is described to be the colour of storm clouds, He is adorned in bright yellow garments that contrast his dusky skin. The yellow garments are called *Pitambari*. He is also often shown wielding His divine discus which is called *Sudarshana Chakra*.

6. The sixth stanza speaks about *Sri Vishnu's* leelas in the form of *Sri Krishna*. *Sri Krishna* was known to steal butter from the houses of *gopis*, earning Him the nickname 'Makkan Chor' or 'stealer of butter'. When the *gopis* would complain about His doing to *Mother Yashoda*, she punished him by tying him to a mortar. *Mother Yashoda* is oblivious to the fact that her little son is none other than the Lord of the Universe, who cannot be bound by anything.

9. Andal's lore

A painting depicting Sri Ranganatha and Devi Andal

In the town of *Srivilliputhur*,
Bhudevi, takes mortal guise
As a gorgeous young maiden,
With lotus eyes and glowing face
She strings garlands
For *Sri Ranganatha*

But she'd adorn herself
With the beautiful garlands
Imagining herself to be his bride
Then devotedly offers them to Him
Impressed by the simple act
He happily accepts the garlands
Worn by the poetess of love
On *Makar Sankranti*
She weds *Ranganatha*
Her love letters to Him
Became revered scriptures
Her words of admiration
Strung into poetry
Her innocent heart
Sang only his praises
Spending hours lost in thought
Her mind centered on Him
She'd pour her heart out
Speaking of longing and separation
Renouncing worldly life
And getting lost in His love
She lived her life in ecstasy
Filled with love and devotion
Before merging with the idol
Of her beloved *Sri Ranganatha*
And returns to her abode *Vaikuntha*
For her love for Him is eternal

- **Poet's note:** This poem has been written after extensive research on *Andal Devi*. As a poet, I have tried my best to capture *Devi Andal's* pure devotion to *Sri Ranganatha* in the form of poetry. But *Devi Andal's* love and devotion for the Lord is unmatched and hence any inaccuracy or mistakes are regretted.

- This poem recounts the life of *Devi Andal*, a poet-saint born in *Srivilliputhur* who is believed to be an incarnation of *Bhudevi* who was found by *Periyalver* (also known as *Vishnuchittar*).

- As a young girl, *Devi Andal* made garlands for *Sri Ranganatha* and wore them herself, imagining she was his bride. Her father initially saw this as disrespectful and stopped her. However, *Sri Ranganatha* refused the fresh garlands and appeared in her father's dream, asking only for the garlands worn by *Devi Andal*. The next day, when she offered the garlands worn by *Devi Andal*, *Sri Ranganatha* accepted them, and they turned into gold.

- *Devi Andal* inspires me as a poet with her deep love and devotion, beautiful writing, and strong emotions. Her work, the *Tiruppavai*, shows how poetry can express deep spiritual feelings. This encourages me to explore emotions and spirituality in my own writing. *Devi Andal's* passion and timeless poems motivate me to write poetry that touches people's hearts.

10. The Divine Guide

Painting depicting Mata Saraswati (The Goddess of Knowledge and Wisdom)

The one who brings light,
To a student's life
Through her valuable teachings,

Is the Goddess of Knowledge Herself
With a pure mind,
The teacher guides
Her students, who are blessed
With the gift of her presence.
I bow to my teacher,
And trust her to lead me
On the righteous path
She illuminates my life
With her brilliance,
Her compassion,
And her wisdom
For me, her presence
Is akin to *Gyanapradayani* herself
As *Saraswati* takes human form
To guide her children,
That form is the TEACHER

Interpretation:

This poem elevates the role of a teacher to that of a divine entity, comparing her to the Goddess of Knowledge, *Saraswati*. The teacher's guidance, compassion, and brilliance are highlighted as transformative, leading students on the path of righteousness. The poem emphasises the sacred bond between teacher and student, suggesting that through her teachings, a teacher embodies the essence of *Saraswati*, nurturing the minds and souls of her students.

11. A Divine Birth

A painting depicting Sri Krishna being carried out of Kamsa's prison just after birth by His father Vasudeva as Ananthasesha protect the two against the rain

In the rainy month of *Bhadrapad,*
The One who cannot be bound,

The one who is boundless

Is born to parents,

Trapped and chained in a prison

He, Who is *Kansa*'s sworn enemy

Is born to avenge his injustice

As the stars and planets align

Nature herself welcomes the child

The skies cry tears of joy

Devi Yamuna, parts her waters

To make way for the brilliant child

Anantashesha shields Him from the rain

As He lies in the basket

His father carrying him to safety

He, a child so divine

Making *Gokul* fall in love with his charm

Playing with friends

And taking cows to graze

As He casts spells with His flute

Enchanting and tricking *Gopis*

Stealing and eating butter

Charming his beloved *Radha*

The little boy, perfect in all aspects

He is the Supreme Lord

He is the darling of *Gokula*

He is *KRISHNA*

- The poem describes the birth of *Sri Krishna*. It speaks of the irony that He, Who is limitless and boundless is born to *Devaki* and *Vasudeva* who are imprisoned by *Devaki's* brother *Kamsa* due to a prophecy that stated that her eighth child would be the reason for his death.

- When *Sri Krishna* is born, *Devaki* and *Vasudeva's* chains miraculously break and the guards fall asleep, which gives them a chance to save their eighth child from a cruel death (as *Kamsa* had killed the previous 7 infants).

- When *Vasudeva* steps out of the prison with *Krishna* in a basket, it is the month of *Bhadrapad*, which is a rainy month in the *Hindu* calendar. While enroute to *Gokul*, the village of his friend *Nanda*, *Vasudeva* has to pass through *Yamuna*, but as he steps into the waters, *Devi Yamuna*, who is personified in the poem, parts the water to create a path for him. *Anantasesha*, the five-headed snake, uses its hoods to shield Sri *Krishna* from the rains as the father and son reach *Gokul*.

- In *Gokul*, *Krishna* is fostered by *Yashoda* and *Nanda* without their knowledge and as a young boy, he enchants the gopis, charms his beloved *Radha* and plays his melodious flute among many of his pastimes.

12. The Fierce Mother

Maa Kali of Dakshineshwar, Bengal

Oh Mother! The fierce One,
Who is Dark as night

Adorned in a garland of skulls
Your hair untame and wild
Wielding the sword
You cut through
The blanket of ignorance
You hold the burning flame
That burns one's ego to ash
Behind her fearsome form
Is the loving Mother
Who protects her children
With an adoring gaze
I look up to You as a Mother
What more can Vibhu say?
I bow to you in pure devotion
And submit myself to You
Trusting your guidance
I shall forever stay
Under your caring gaze
Oh sweet Mother!
Accept my offering
Of red hibiscus flowers
As I weave my devotion
Into a garland of flowers

- The poem is a heartfelt ode to the divine Mother Goddess often called *Maa Kali*. She described with dark skin, untamed hair wielding a sword which is figuratively used to cut through the blanket of ignorance that surrounds her devotees.

- Although her appearance is described to be fierce and fearsome, Vibhu describes her as a loving Mother with a loving gaze upon her children who keeps her children protected and in Her shelter. She guides her children on the righteous path as the devotee completely submits themselves to Her.

- Vibhu finally concludes asking *Maa Kali* to accept the offering of red hibiscus flowers which are known to be *Maa Kali*'s favourite flower. The red hibiscus flowers symbolize the devotee's devotion and submission to the Goddess.

13. The Endless Search

Chanchala is another name of Devi Radha, which translates to restless because Devi Radha's eyes are constantly searching for Krishna, Her beloved

I'm stuck in an endless search
I roamed the mountains
I sailed across seas
I searched the forests,
I seeked You behind the trees

I sought you in cities
I visited temples
I sat in churches
I prayed in mosques
All in vain,
I couldn't find Her,
I had lost
But as She revealed Herself,
I found Her in my heart,
Residing in me
She was always there
With me the whole time
My playful Mother!

- The poem describes a devotees search for the Divine Mother far and wide through mountains forests and seas, in the cities, temples, churches and mosques. But the devotee unable to find Her, is upset and considers to have lost in the game of hide and seek with the Divine Mother. When the devotee gives up, the playful Mother reveals herself to be residing nowhere but the devotees own heart, within the devotee.

- In conclusion, the poem expresses the realization that the Divine Mother shouldn't be searched for in the physical world but rather she resides within oneself and should be sought in one's heart. If seeked for in the correct place the playful, loving nature of the Mother is always with them.

14. Ram! The Sacred Name

Bhakta Hanuman with Sri Ram, Devi Sita and Lakshmana

Ram! The sacred Name
That *Hanuman* chants
Loosing Himself in devotion

Ram! The sacred Name
Hanuman dances in bliss
As the Name reaches His ears
Ram! The sacred Name
Chanting it is above all
The best form of worship
Ram! The sacred Name
It is the wealth
That makes a beggar rich
Ram! The sacred Name
Vibhu challenges thieves
To steal this wealth
Ram! The sacred Name
It is the wealth
That can never be stolen
Ram! The sacred name
It is the divine Name,
That is greater than *Ram* Himself

- The poem celebrates the power and beauty of the sacred name '*Ram*'. It describes how *Hanuman*, *Lord Ram*'s devoted follower, finds joy and bliss in simply hearing and chanting the name. The poem highlights that chanting '*Ram*' is the highest form of worship.

- The poem emphasizes that the sacred name of *Lord Ram* is a spiritual wealth. A kind of wealth that makes even a poor person rich in devotion and fulfillment. Unlike material riches, it cannot be lost or stolen. The poem expresses the belief that *Lord Ram*'s name holds more power than *Lord Ram* himself, showing the immense significance of chanting it with devotion.

Disclaimer:
This poem has been written after taking inspiration from a *Doha* by *Sant Kabir Das* called '*Ram Naam Ki Loot Hai Loot Sake Toh Loot*'.

Author's Note

As we come to the end of this collection of poems, I want to take a moment to express my deepest gratitude to all those who have played a part in bringing this book to life. First and foremost, I am thankful to the readers—each of you who has taken the time to engage with these words, allowing them to resonate with your own experiences. Your support and appreciation have made this journey all the more meaningful.

This collection represents a year of reflection, growth, and creativity. In the course of writing these poems, I have explored the themes of faith, spirituality, and the search for understanding, and I am grateful for the opportunity to share these thoughts with you. What began as an experiment in expression has grown into something far more significant, andI feel truly fortunate to have had the opportunity and space to create something meaningful.

As I look to the future, I can't help but feel a sense of hope and excitement for what's to come. The journey of spiritual growth and creative expression is never truly finished, and I look forward to continuing to write and deepen my understanding of the Divine. My hope is to craft poetry that not only captures my evolving thoughts and experiences but that also invites you, the reader, to join me on this journey of discovery and reflection.

In every poem, I have strived to capture the essence of something beyond myself—an attempt to understand the Divine and the world around me. As I continue to grow spiritually, I hope to write more poems that are richer in wisdom, deeper in insight, and as I continue on this journey, my hope is that my writing will grow and become more aligned with the deeper truths I discover along the way.

Thank you again for being part of this process, for allowing these poems to become part of your own spiritual journey, and for the encouragement that keeps me writing. The path ahead is one of exploration, and I am excited to continue this adventure, not only for myself but alongside all of you.